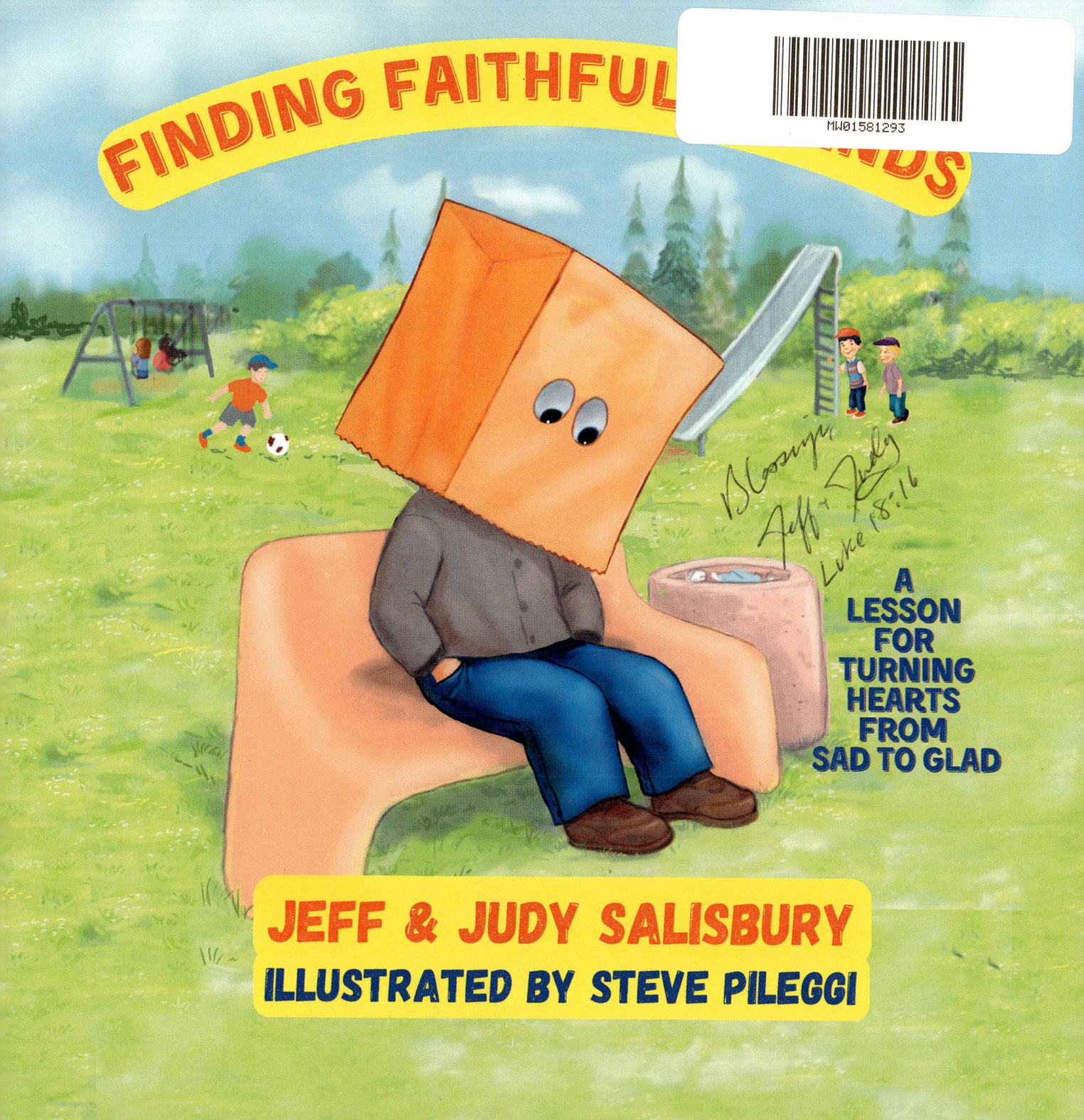

Finding Faithful Friends:
A Lesson for Turning Hearts from Sad to Glad
Written by Jeff & Judy Salisbury
Illustrated by Steve Pileggi

Copyright © 2023 by Jeff & Judy Salisbury.
Published by Logos Presentations, Woodland, WA 98674
www.logospresentations.com

Library of Congress Control Number: 2023902826

Scripture quotations taken from the New American Standard Bible Updated, © 1960, 1962, 1963, 1968, 1971, 1972, 1973, 1975, 1977, 1995 by The Lockman Foundation. Used by permission.

All rights reserved. No part of this publication may be reproduced, stored in a retrieval system, or transmitted in any form or by any means—electronic, mechanical, digital, photocopy, recording, or any other without the prior permission of Logos Presentations.

Printed in the United States of America. **ISBN: 978-0-9657678-2-8**

IN LOVING MEMORY
OF LARRY "GRANDPA" SALISBURY

AND TO ALL THOSE WHO REALIZED THEY SHOULD IMPACT THE LIVES OF OTHERS FOR GOOD.

On a bench at the park one fine, sunshiny summer day, sat a lonely little boy who just wanted to play.

Daily, his sadness continued to grow as the other children played in the soft grass below.

"No one, no never, do they ask me to play, but even if they did, they would probably laugh AT me, saying I just don't fit in."

It belonged to his Grandpa, whom he loved very much. He knew that his Grandpa wouldn't mind if he touched.

As he dug and he searched, to his surprise, in that box there, he found all of Grandpa's supplies.

As a clown in the circus many years ago,
Grandpa brought joy to others,
and made their happy smiles grow.

Looking over the items, the little boy thought, "If I painted my face like a clown with a grin, then I could share tricks, and maybe I would fit in."

"I could juggle and do special tricks for them too, perhaps then they would like me after seeing all I can do!"

The more that he practiced, the better he got, "Grandpa would be so proud and so pleased," the little boy thought.

On the day of the carnival, he had quite a few fears, he felt like not going, afraid there'd be jeers.

"I made a promise; I said I'd be there.
If I don't show up now,
they'll all think I don't care."

"NO!" The little boy said with a firm and loud voice, "I signed up and I told them that this was my choice."

He applied the clown make-up, his face he did hide, thinking no one would know him, he felt satisfied.

The little boy arrived at the carnival spot
when he saw all those people, it sure felt like a lot.
After just a few minutes, his turn soon came.
Ready or not, they called out his name!

Then that one became two.

He tossed in a third, and he hopped, and he turned, the little boy did his best to remember all he had learned!

It didn't take long before the laughter began.
But the laughter was WITH him, and that was his plan.

Seeing their smiling faces as they clapped and they cheered,
the little boy knew it was silly to fear.
The joy that he gave them made his heart so glad,
he knew bringing joy to others meant he didn't have to be sad.

The next day, without the costume, clown makeup, or tricks, the little boy quietly strolled to the park bench that he always picks.

When all the children saw him
even before he could sit,
they ran to him,
feeling free to admit,
that they would also feel lonely and blue,
but the joy that he showed them
made them joyful too!

Some children told him that he was so brave to stand up before everyone; it would make them afraid! But as he juggled and did his tricks with a grin, they thought their fear could leave them, just as it left him!

Just then, he knew that they all really cared;
they had so much in common,
he then proudly declared that he no longer felt sad, alone, and not smart;
reaching out to help others is the best place to start.

It wasn't the tricks that made him well-loved,
it was using his talent from the One up above,
Who gave him the chance to see what is true,
bringing happiness to others made him happy too.

With great joy in his heart, he then made up his mind, to be the best friend he could be all of the time.

To lift other hearts he never imagined he'd see as afraid as his once was but will never again be.

"Dear Jesus, thank You for giving me what I needed to bring happiness to others, it's such a simple thing. I'm sorry I was silly believing what wasn't true about me and those children, who are just like me too. To help make people joyful is what I will do, Being a good friend to all and especially to You!"

"I purchased this book for a friend, before giving the book to her, I decided to read it. I am a senior citizen and have been having a rough time, similar to Ditzy. I lost my husband last fall, was unexpected. So I have had the same feeling: like being alone, will I get over this and such things. Ditzy had the same feeling, but The Good Shepard came and rescued her. The same thing happened to me, thank God for The Good Shepard and many good friends. Just because this is a book for a young person, don't think it cannot open your eyes (very wide). Thank you, Judy Salisbury, for writing this, and please give it a read no matter your age."

**PEGGY FARRINGTON
5-STAR AMAZON REVIEWER**

"This is a wonderful story for all ages. I sent it to my granddaughter, age 5. When asked, my son told me that they had read it for the last five nights. My daughter called a family night and, with a little protest, read it to her three teenage sons. They all enjoyed it! What a wonderful way to tell of Jesus' love. This is such a sweet lesson without being 'preachy.' The illustrations are absolutely fantastic!"

**VERIFIED PURCHASER
5-STAR AMAZON REVIEWER**

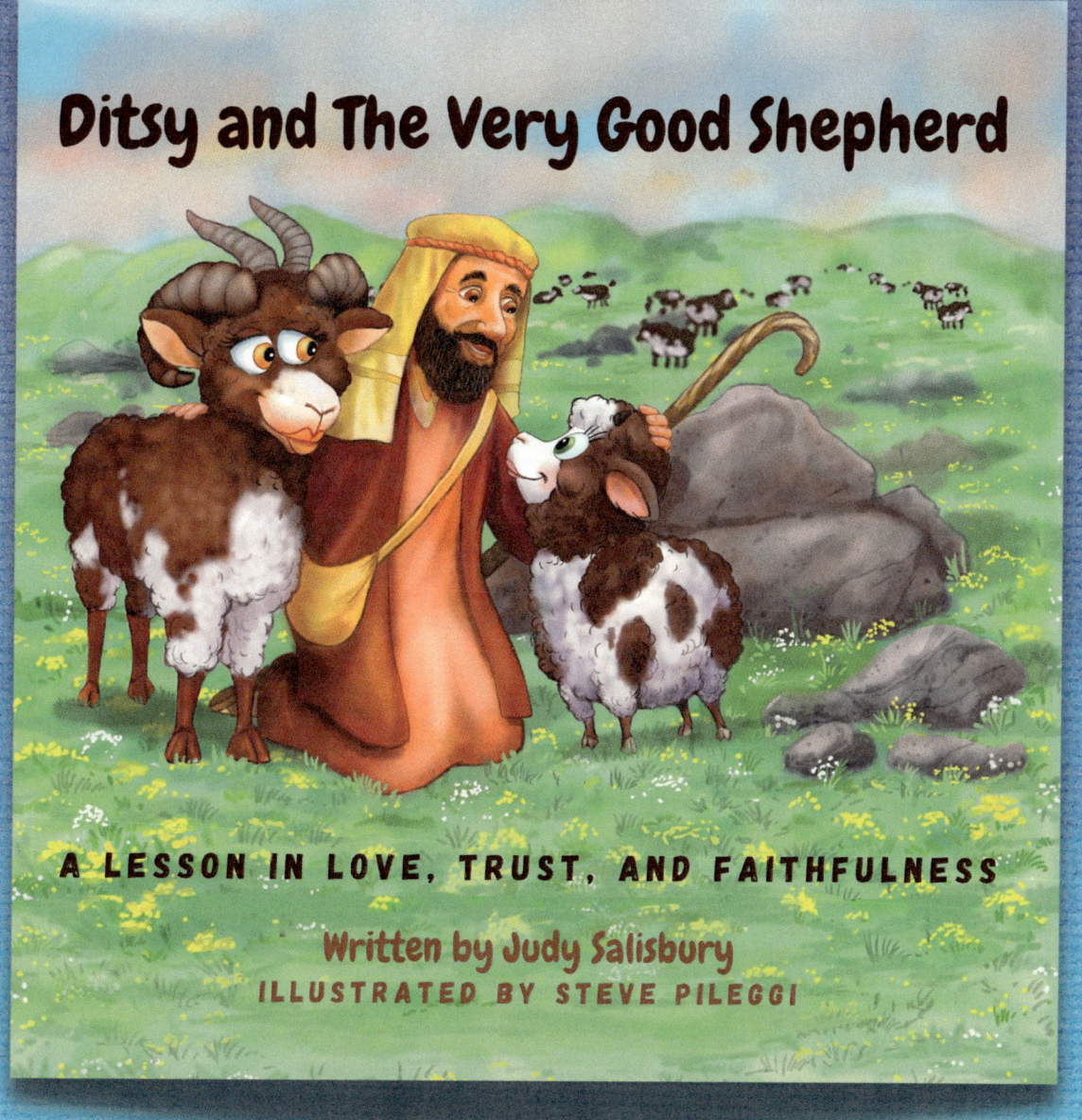

FIND DITSY AND OTHER RESOURCES AND INFORMATION AT:
WWW.LOGOSPRESENTATIONS.COM
ALL RESOURCES AVAILABLE NOW ON AMAZON

"I know of no book on the market that better meets the spiritual needs and fills the intellectual hunger of women who want to see their friends, family, and children in the kingdom of God."

—From the Foreword
DR. NORMAN L. GEISLER
author or co-author of over one-hundred books,
Co-founder of Veritas International University

The first book for women on Christian Apologetics, and the first book women turn to for Christian Apologetics.

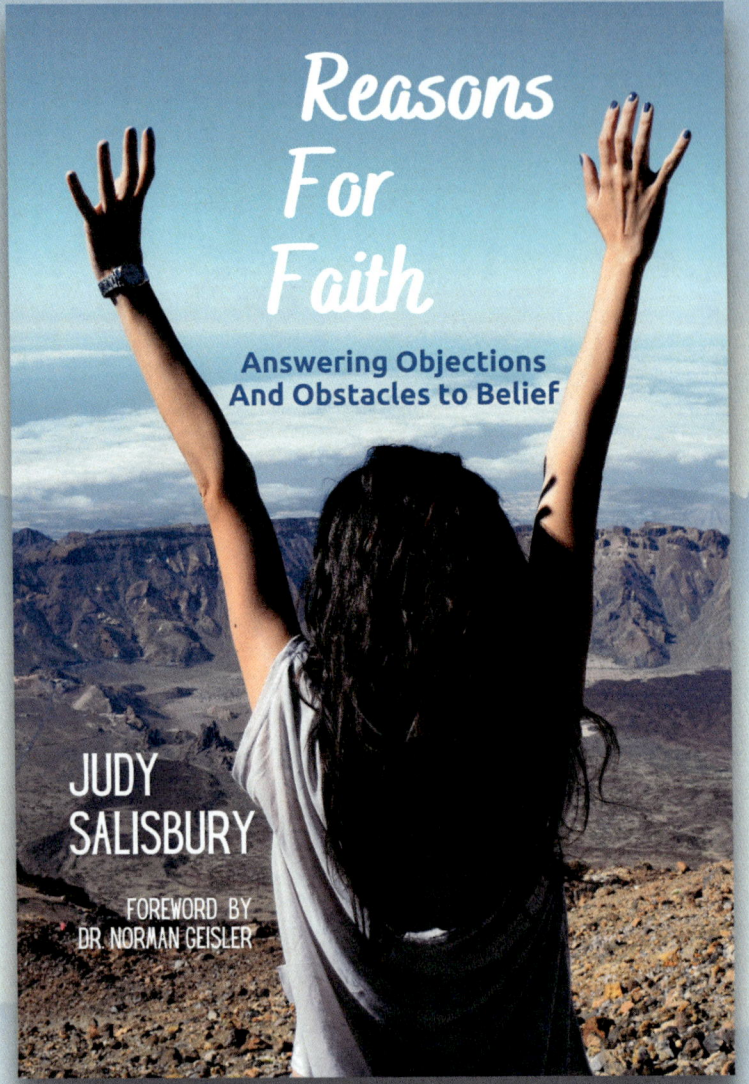

Reasons For Faith
Answering Objections And Obstacles to Belief

JUDY SALISBURY

FOREWORD BY DR. NORMAN GEISLER

"A powerful tool for the defense of the faith, one that combines fascinating facts with true spiritual understanding and a refreshing sense of humor."

—JILL MARTIN RISCHE
Co-founder of Walter Martin's Religious InfoNet
and co-author of *Through the Windows of Heaven*

Engaging Encounters

Your Guide to Apply Reasons for Faith

Judy Salisbury

FOREWORD BY DR. DAVID GEISLER

"Absorbing, instructional, insightful… It's an apologetics manual wrapped in a warm blanket. Snuggle up with it."

Julie Loos, Director,
Ratio Christi Boosters

"Over the last 15 years, I have had the privilege to pass on to students many of the things that I've learned from my father, Norm Geisler, in the area of apologetics and evangelism. But in all those years, I've met very few people who are truly skilled at integrating their apologetic knowledge in their witness in ways that are personally, culturally, and even religiously sensitive. Yet I was pleasantly surprised to learn that Judy Salisbury can do all that and more!"

Dr. David Geisler
President/Co-Founder,
Norm Geisler
International Ministries

(FROM THE FOREWORD)

THE EMMAUS CONVERSATION

An Eyewitness Account
From the Unnamed Disciple

JUDY SALISBURY

"The Emmaus Conversation brings to life that famous encounter between the two disciples and our Lord Jesus on the road to Emmaus. While it is based in part on an imaginative reconstruction, it is filled with the throbbing pulse of the excitement of the sensational impact that our Lord's resurrection should have on all of our lives."

Dr. WALTER C. KAISER, Jr.,
President Emeritus Gordon-Conwell Theological Seminary

"Judy's touching, sensitive, and creative retelling of the Emmaus road account stands in a class by itself. She handily employs theological insight by connecting the Old and New Testaments. This she does, not through bland exposition, but by unpacking its particulars, and by lacing her narrative with colorful and creative conversation."

Dr. JEFFREY L. SEIF
Distinguished Professor of Bible and Jewish Studies, Kings University

---

"Judy Salisbury has a way, like no other, to take us back in time on the road to Emmaus. Through *The Emmaus Conversation*, she beautifully and creatively unfolds an extraordinary dialogue that brings out scriptural insights, and spiritual progression. The Emmaus Conversation can't help but change hearts. A must read for all."

DONNA MORLEY
Co-founder Faith & Reason Forum

"I found *The Emmaus Conversation* remarkable and riveting. Judy Salisbury portrays Yeshua in such a beautiful, gentle, perfect way. Tears were rolling down my face as I envisioned him through her words. She did a fantastic job with the Scriptures, networking them all together with profound significance—the mark of a seasoned apologist. The book, as a whole, is fascinating, captivating, eye-opening, and doctrinally sound. I also think it would make an awesome movie. The Lord's hand was definitely in this project. I can't wait for my Jewish friends to read it!"

JENNIFER SANDS, author, speaker, 9/11 Widow

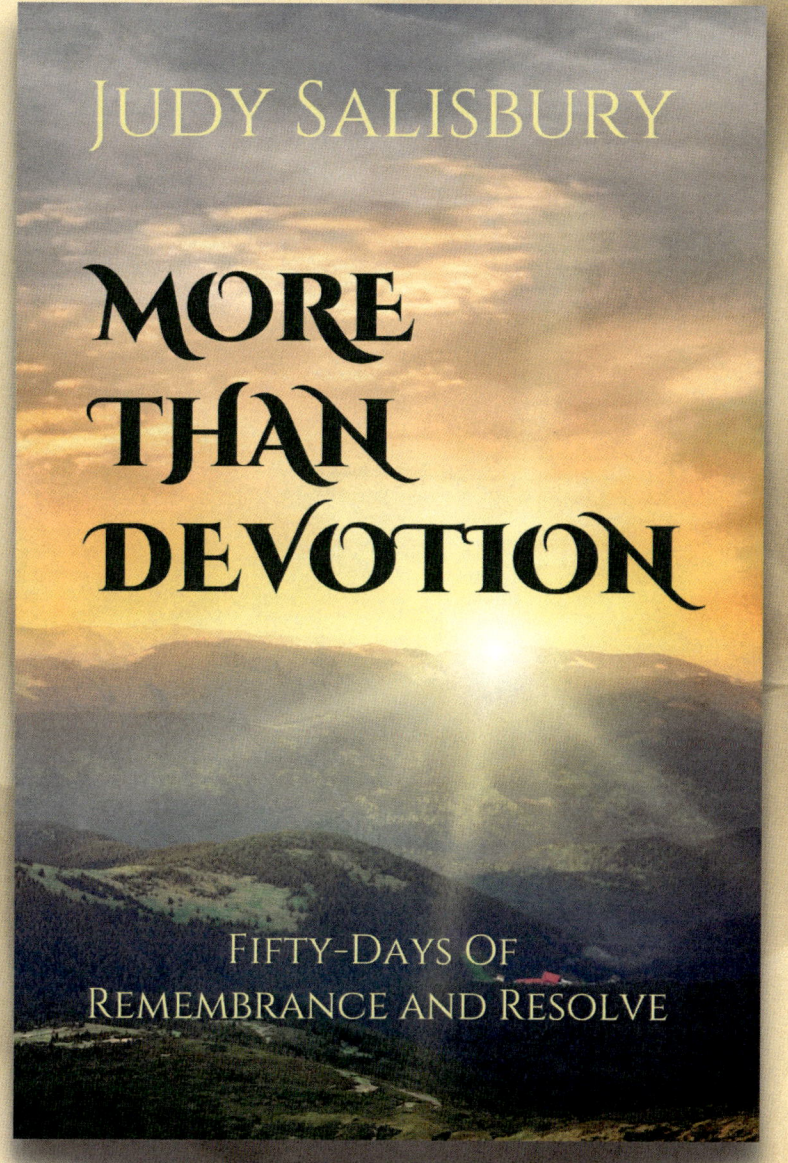

Whether you are a new believer or have walked with the Lord for many years, *More Than Devotion* provides fifty opportunities to learn through various biblical personalities and their circumstances.

As you read each day's related accounts from the Old and New Testaments, you will realize that God is the same yesterday, today, and forever. You will also see that human nature appears unchanging without God's intervention, making this work relatable and relevant.

With the backdrop of remembrance, each day provides a practical application and an achievable call to action, allowing fifty opportunities to move forward with significant personal and spiritual growth.

Judy Salisbury, in this book, provides an oasis for ministry leaders or lay Christians alike. She interweaves stories, Scripture, theology, and applicable lessons that we can use in our lives. I encourage the reader to take time as they read and drink from the fountain of God's Word here in her 50-days of refreshing.

THOMAS F. MARSHALL, D.MIN, ThD, Minister, Author, Christian Educator, Chaplain, Board Certified Pastoral Counselor

Made in the USA
Monee, IL
17 May 2023

33455181R00029